Memories of Manteo
And Roanoke Island, N.C.

by Suzanne Tate
as told by Cora Mae Basnight

NAGS HEAD ART
Illustrations by James Melvin

Nags Head Art, Publisher
P.O. Box 88
Nags Head, N.C. 27959

Library of Congress Catalog Number 88-60590
ISBN 0-9616344-2-1
Copyright© 1988 by Nags Head Art

ALL RIGHTS RESERVED
PRINTED IN THE UNITED STATES OF AMERICA
FIRST EDITION

Dedicated to Moncie L. Daniels, Sr.
Frugal, industrious and conscientious
leader of his community.

CORA MAE BASNIGHT
photo by Foster Scott
[courtesy of *The Lost Colony*]

INTRODUCTION

My friendship with Cora Mae Basnight grew out of mutual commiseration. By chance, we were hospital mates at the old Albemarle Hospital in Elizabeth City, North Carolina, 28 years ago. She was recuperating from surgery; I had been hospitalized following an auto accident. I was feeling blue, and "Cora Mae, the Clown"—in her wonderful way—helped me out of my depression.

She has entertained thousands in her role as Agona, an Indian squaw, in *The Lost Colony*, the outdoor drama presented every summer on Roanoke Island, North Carolina. Cora Mae holds the record for playing the same role longer than any other actress in American theater—25 years!

In *Memories of Manteo*, the third of my oral history series, Cora Mae will entertain you in her inimitable way.

Suzanne Tate

CORA MAE—age 6
with Mama [Belva Daniels]

DOWN-HOMER

Cora Mae Basnight is my name. I am a "down-homer" just like my Daddy and Mama, Moncie and Belva Daniels. A down-homer doesn't have e-go-tis-tic—how do you say it? Egotistical ways.

Material things meant nothing to Daddy. He was used to a hard life when growing up, and he respected any person who worked with his hands.

The employees at his store would give him clothes at Christmas as he wouldn't buy anything for himself. Mama used to tease Daddy that he was not used to anything anyway—that he had been raised in a Wanchese fish camp.

So that people wouldn't think that he was stuckup, Daddy only dressed up for a funeral. He never missed one of those.

They named a bridge here in Manteo after me, but they shouldn't have. There already was a road named for me—Agona—after the part that I played in *The Lost Colony*. A woman came up to me one time and said, "Oh, you're the famous Cora Mae—you have a bridge and a street named for you!" It embarrassed me to death.

FROG CONCERT

My yard used to be a wild pond full of marsh grass. There were goslings swimming in the pond and willows hanging over it with trunks as big around as a fat woman.

When I sat on my porch, the light from Bodie Island Lighthouse would shine at my feet. I thought it was the most beautiful place in the world.

The pond is gone now, but we used to have a frog concert every night. There were Mama and Daddy frogs and little fellows. The Daddy frogs would go "Under Root, Under Root," Mama frogs would go "Ribbet, Ribbet," and the little ones would say "Fry Bacon, Fry Bacon." When you heard the three together, it made a wonderful concert.

I would love to have a tape of that frog concert. I studied music for ten years and never heard better.

When my children were young, I would rock them, read a story and tell them to sing like the frogs. The children would go to sleep listening to them.

I warned all the men in town—"Don't you dare get my frogs!" But one night somebody gigged them all. When Mr. Morgan, the health officer, came to Manteo, he made us fill up the pond with sand to get rid of mosquitoes and pollution.

BABYSITTING EXPERT

Like the old lady in the shoe, I sat here and had seven kids—E.J., Dottie, Sally, Sarah, Junior, Della and Marc. I rocked all of them and my grandchildren, too.

It spoiled me to stay home all the time. I have always loved it and especially liked to work in my yard.

Since I was 19, I have never been without a child. They all paid me to take care of the grandchildren so it gave me a little job on the side. I was well qualified for babysitting!

THE BACK ROAD

No streets were laid off in Manteo when I was growing up. There were just four dirt roads. Agona—that I live on—was a crooked one that everybody called "The Back Road."

There were big holes in the roads that caused a buggy to go up and down—"dippity-do". Mr. Carson Davis had a 3-seater carriage that was the most elegant in town. It had springs and a top with fringe all around it and was drawn by his horse, Prince. Every

Saturday a man named Joe Sykes, who worked for Mr. Davis, would comb Prince's tail with a long brush so that it would look beautiful for Sunday drives.

Mr. Davis and his wife Miss Ella always rode in the front of the carriage, with the children—Ralph, Vernon and Ann—in the back. I rode with them through the woods on the crooked dirt road to Ft. Raleigh one Sunday. It was really a beautiful sight.

ON THE WATERFRONT

We lived in the big house next to the Davis', but I was raised up on the waterfront!

I grew up there with Balfour Baum. His father, Washington Baum, had a house and store on the waterfront. The family lived upstairs. Everybody liked Wash Baum. He was a Sunday School teacher, judge and country philosopher.

Boats came in and tied up at wharves in front of Wash Baum's store. I liked to watch them come in with their catches of fish. When the boats were going out, I could hear them while I was lying in bed and could recognize each one of them by the sound of their "putt-putt".

There was a time when the Manteo waterfront was a bad environment with men cussing and talking dirty and doing a lot of drinking. I have seen men lying halfway down the wharves, bottles in hand, and others drunk in their boats.

Woodie Fearing remembers well the time when he was only 12 years old that he broke up a fight between two drunk fishermen. One afternoon he was working on the waterfront shaving up 300-pound blocks of ice with a big shaver made of one-quarter inch steel. The weight of the thing helped shave the ice. It was eight or ten inches wide with 3-inch triangular points.

Young Woodie was at the fishhouse when some men came in with run boats used to bring fish to market. While their catch was being unloaded, the fishermen went off and bought a bottle from the liquor store and nearly finished it.

Back at the fishhouse, they got into an argument as they were well under the influence of the bottle's contents. When Woodie's Uncle Jim stepped in to separate the two, one of the fishermen resented it and grabbed a fish knife. He then turned toward Woodie's Daddy who was also standing nearby.

Right away, Woodie—holding the ice shaver waist-high—jumped between his Daddy and the fishermen. That shaver could have made a terrific wound; it stopped the quarrel and the fishermen quickly left the waterfront.

BOOTLEGGING GALORE

There used to be liquor and drunks everywhere when I was a girl. Five bootleggers lived in Manteo, selling white lightning here.

Most of the bootleg whiskey was made in East Lake and Buffalo City to the west of Manteo. Sheriff Frank Cahoon—who was born and raised in East Lake—said that the people there didn't see anything wrong in making whiskey.

One bootlegger moved over from East Lake to Manteo and made liquor right in his kitchen. The man stole from our woodpile for his operation. Daddy said that he couldn't keep any wood!

Another bootlegger had a barn full of liquor right downtown. Some friends and I played "hooky" from school one day and stayed in the barn with a girlfriend who handed out "packages" [bottles of liquor] to customers while her father was out-of-town.

The bootleggers liked to have a woman riding with them when making deliveries so their trips would be less likely to look suspicious. I have ridden many times with bootleggers—I rode for the excitement and adventure of it.

Daddy owned the "Toot-n-Tell-It", a local juke joint, which stood near the curve at the midway intersection south of Manteo. One day I was with a fellow on the way to the Toot-n-Tell-It to deliver white lightning at the back door. We thought we saw a "revy-noo-er" coming so we hid in a ditch behind a potato barn.

MACK

Daddy told the story that there used to be a town character named Mack Horney [McHorney Midgett]. He was a slow-learner who loved his firewater.

One time when he drank too much they threw him in jail. But they had to beat him up before they put him in there. "Where did you get your liquor from?" they asked Mack. He stuttered that he was not going to tell on N-N-Nut. That was the nickname of the bootlegger!

Daddy said that Mack headed to Oregon Inlet on his horse one day and was going down the Banks [Hatteras Island] to sell white lightning. He jumped in the water and swam across Oregon Inlet with his horse, and tied to his horse's neck was a suitcase full of liquor!

THE HOT-RODDER

I started playing the devil when I was about 13 years old. At 14, I was on the road with my Model T coupe—you didn't have to have a license back then.

I was a hot-rodder, and I had a lot of fun. In my Model T, I jumped the holes in the roads—every one of them.

Daddy had an oil and gas business so all I had to do was run up to his tanks and fill up whenever I wanted to. There were not many cars in town, but they got off the road right quick when they saw me coming!

When I was a little older, I drove Daddy's 8-cylinder Hudson. I was racing with Ralph Davis one day on the road to Wanchese. On the first sharp curve I went right down into an old dipping vat for cattle and right up out of it as it was full of leaves. I don't know why I didn't get killed!

Several years later, I rode with my husband Saint [Basnight] when he was delivering groceries to welfare people. Saint stopped in

Colington at a pretty little house with a picket fence, and I asked the man there if he knew anyone in Manteo. He said that he knew the cop, George Twiford, who had told him about a young girl in Manteo who had run him crazy—she ran him off the road with her Model T.

That girl was me. We used to play with the cops. Cop Twiford would stand in the road with his arms out for me to stop, but I would keep on coming through. I knew that he would jump aside!

BEATING THE TOLL

In 1927, each person used to be charged a toll of 25¢ to cross the bridge over Roanoke Sound. That was when the bridge was first built. In order to beat the toll some of us would hide in the rumble seat of my Model-T.

One time Rondal Lewark and I were shut up in there, and the others could not open the seat when we arrived on the other side of the bridge. We had to ride all the way to Kitty Hawk before they could get us out.

We were headed for the Soundside Pavilion where Capt. Dan Hayman ran a dance hall. I thought that we would smother before we got there!

BUSH-WHACKING

At a place known as Tall Timbers—on the other side of the island—we used to drive fast through the woods on sandy trails. We called it "bush-whacking" as bushes would hit the side of the car.

When Goldie Meekins came here in the late 20's, she said that she would hear us say, "I saw you bush-whacking last night." She wondered what we were talking about!

GOOD TIMES

We used to have good times in the 20's on hayrides to Ft. Raleigh. That was before it was a national historic site.

The boys would fill up a truck with straw. Hazel Willis—who was full of music—played the ukelele, and we sang going down the road.

There was a long wharf at Ft. Raleigh for public use. We went swimming and picnicking on the shore.

One time when we were up there swimming, Sam Griffin lost his false teeth. He dove right down to the bottom of the sound and found his teeth and slapped them right in his mouth. We were all so surprised!

Camille Brinkley's folks had watermelon parties for us and fish fries on the shore of their farm. We had happy days over there at the Brinkley's. They were good to young people and were always entertaining us.

Mr. Brinkley joined us in good times. He liked to tease us. One night Camille and I went "scivvy-dipping"—swimming in our underwear. When we came back to the shore, our clothes were gone. Camille's Daddy had hidden them. At first he teased us that he was going to tell her mother; then he threw us our clothes.

We all enjoyed riding around in cars just for the fun of it. There were salesmen coming and going, trying to sell automobiles. We rode with a lot of drummers.

A man we called Pop arrived in town when I was about 14. He was a drifter—we didn't know anything about where he came from. Pop took us for rides in his touring car, and we had a lot of fun.

HIDING OUT

One night when we were in our teens, Delia Peele and I wanted to go out and ride around with our friends. She could go if I could go, but Mama said *no*—that I'd been out enough.

So it made me mad, and I hid out under the front doorsteps. After I got there, I was scared to come out because Mama had everybody in cars looking for me. Cars were roaring everywhere, and the bigger the crowd became, the more scared I was to move.

When daylight arrived, I knew that I had to come out from hiding. Mama thought that I was dead so I came out at the right time! She was so glad to see me that she didn't say another word.

ICE PLANT ISLAND

I used to enjoy listening to the noise of the plant making ice on Ice Plant Island. It sounded like "Bam, Bam," night and day, but it didn't bother me.

Our parents took us swimming around the point of Ice Plant Island where there was a wide, sandy beach. There was a little bathhouse on the point. Carson Davis had a sign there for years—"Davis Wants to See You."

It was really lovely on Ice Plant Island. Sometimes we had picnics there.

JERRY-THE SHIPWRECKED DOG

When the big cargo ship *Elizabeth* shipwrecked at Rodanthe, I was only 9 years old. It was the first big ship I ever saw.

Uncle Dory, Mama's brother, was in charge of the salvage. I'll never forget the shoes—black patent leather with white buttons down the side—that he gave me from off the ship. They were soaking wet with saltwater so they didn't last too long.

There was a big St. Bernard dog on the ship. Uncle Dory took him home to his children who named the dog Jerry. He was so big that the children rode him all over the yard. Uncle Dory built a cart and hooked up Jerry to it. My cousin Theodore rode in it uptown.

Theodore would slip in the kitchen and get biscuits for Jerry. The dog gulped whole biscuits one at a time until there were no biscuits left for the family.

FISH STORM

One time when I was a girl, a waterspout—miniature tornado—came along and sucked up a lot of fish from the sound. It dropped them on the Brinkley Farm south of where I live.

The news went around like wildfire, and everybody ran to the Brinkley Farm with a dishpan to pick up the fish. There was a big crowd there catching the live fish that were just a'popping on the ground.

FIRST AIRPLANE SIGHTED

At the time of World War I, Mama saw the first airplane fly over Manteo. "Young'uns, get under the house," she said. "The Kaiser has sent the Germans to blow us all off the earth!" I will never forget it as long as I live.

The plane landed on the shore in front of the Brinkley farm, and everybody went to see it. A lot of people were whispering about them being spies.

We were very suspicious of strangers. If we didn't recognize a person walking past the house, we thought that he was either a drummer [salesman] or a German spy.

MY WILD BEACH PONY

When I was 12 years old, Daddy got a beach pony for me. Ponies ran the beach, and anybody who could rope one could have one. Somebody in Willie Jolliff's family tried to train my pony, but no one really got the wildness out of him.

One time he threw me over his head, and I landed right on my feet. Delia Poole, one of my classmates, saw all of that and went to school saying that I was a trick-rider. But it was a piece of luck! Most of the time I fell flat on my back when my pony threw me.

One Sunday afternoon I was headed for Camille Brinkley's when I met Harold Bruce and Wally and Willy who were riding big horses. They made fun of my pony, but I raced them and beat. I also told them that I could ride up a big sandhill, and they laughed at that . But I left them standing while I galloped uphill.

I had a lot of happy days with my wild beach pony.

SCHOOL DAYS AND SWITCHES

Sometimes you had mean teachers. When I was in the third grade, I had one like that. She would beat us if one foot or toe was sticking out in the aisle. Then she would laugh after she did it.

Every little thing you did was wrong. Coy Tillett got switched for wading in his boots at recess. The teacher had told us that if anybody went wading, they would get a beating.

When Coy went home for lunch, he had stripes on his legs from the switching. Miss Emma, his mother, was so mad that she came back to school with him. She called the teacher out of the room and grabbed her by the hair of her head and slung her around!

Another teacher was always telling me, "You never get that arithmetic right—you don't study enough." One day she told us that if anybody passed in a bad paper, they would be switched.

When it came time for me to get it, I grabbed a chair and said, "You come one step closer, and I will let you have it!" Then I threw the chair down and ran home. Mama didn't scold me. She had said that she would finish off anybody who put a hand on me at school.

Most teachers had their hands full. Preston Midgett could always think up mischief. He wrote CACKLE on one side of his desk and YELLOW HEN on the other side. Miss Essie Wescott would make him take it off, but he would get chalk and put it back.

One time she broke seven switches on Preston. She was so weak afterwards that she had to put her head down on her desk to rest.

COUNTY COMMENCEMENT

We used to have a big County Commencement once a year at the old schoolhouse. Young people came from other places in the county—Stumpy Point, Rodanthe and all around. They stayed in homes here as it was too long a trip for them to go back home. They came by boat as there were no ferries or bridges back then.

Miss Mabel Evans organized the County Commencement. There were foot races and speaking contests and story-telling. A band from Elizabeth City came and played.

When I was in the 4th grade, I told a story at school and won. Then I went to the County Commencement to tell it, but I didn't win there. I shed a few tears to know that I had lost.

I didn't win the story-telling contest, but I came in second in the foot races.

WHITE-FACE MINSTREL

There is a black section in Manteo that has been called California for over a hundred years. Cora Scarborough who died recently at the age of 104 said that it was called that when she moved there at the age of 7. No one seems to know how it came to be known as California.

When I was a little girl we went there to the black schoolhouse to a show they put on. The actors powdered all they could to look white—their faces looked like they fell out of a flour barrel. They acted like white folks and dressed like us with ruffled skirts and bows on their hair. Mama's cook said the next day, "Did you see yourself last night?"

We were always invited to see their schoolhouse programs, and they came to our programs at the white school. They were the best singers and actors in the world.

DAVIS BOATS

When I was young, I played with Vernon and Ralph Davis as they lived next door. They always called me "Skinny."

The Davis brothers used to have a boatbuilding business, and they started out in it when they were just children.

In front of our houses, there were deep ditches that were often flooded by rains. One day Vernon and Ralph took the works out of an old clock and put the motor in a little boat they built, and ran it up and down the ditches.

Later their Daddy built a barn for the boys to work in and bought tools and equipment for them. They were always considered to be good boatbuilders.

VILLAGE BLACKSMITH

I remember well Mr. Albert Evans, the blacksmith. When he worked, you could see his strong arms, and all over town you could hear him striking his anvil.

Mr. Albert was also the town undertaker. Bodies were embalmed in a house next to his home. Then they were taken to people's homes. His wife did the shirring—pleating of the material—in the caskets.

One of my favorite poems when I was a schoolgirl was "The Village Blacksmith." I loved poetry and memorized the ones I liked. My inspiration for memorizing that poem, I'm sure, was knowing Mr. Albert.

NAMING CHILDREN

Mama's father was Capt. Thomas P. Midgette. He was from Rodanthe, and was a captain in the Lighthouse Service.

Grandpa named Mama after Belva Lockwood, a Republican, who was one of the first women to run for President of the United

States. But Mama turned out to be a hot Democrat! She had no choice as Daddy was chairman of the local Democrats for years.

Daddy's name was picked out of a book—Monsieur Le Brant, a Frenchman. I don't know why my Grandpa Daniels picked him, but Daddy changed his name to Moncie because he got teased about it at school.

BELVA'S HAPPY DAYS

Mama said that the happiest days in her life was when she went fishing. She lived around the water all of her life and was an outgoing outdoorsman. She loved to go fishing and would go everyday if someone would go with her.

The sun got her bad as she stayed outdoors so much. She got wrinkled up, and Daddy said that she looked like an East Lake alligator!

One day Mama and her friends, Anges Midgett and Mary Mann, came in from fishing. Mama, who was always proud of her figure, said, "I was casting my line today, and the Yankee sportsmen nearby whistled at me. 'Look at that figure!' they said."

She kept on fishing for a compliment until Daddy had an answer: "Well, they'd have to sack your face first!" Then Mama went after him like lightning.

SUNDAY SCHOOL AND CHURCH

There were two churches in town—one Baptist and one Methodist—when I was growing up. Every child went to Sunday School whether their parents did or not. The children were all dressed up in hats with cherries and flowers and ribbons hanging on them.

Ras Wescott's mother, Miss Odessa, had a millinery shop where everybody bought their hats for special occasions like Christmas and Easter. You had to be all ready for spring-time and winter church-going.

One time in the Methodist Church where we went, the preacher was jumping up and down in the pulpit. Finally he ended with "Glory to God!" and jumped clear off his feet. My brother Moncie was little—about 3 years old—and he jumped up just like the preacher and quoted right behind him, "Glory to God!" Everybody laughed, and it broke up the meeting.

The preachers would "take up" on you—preach about the bad things you did, but didn't name any names. However, everybody knew everybody so you knew who he was talking about. The preacher took his text on me quite often!

Ras would pinch us through the chair—got you this morning, didn't he? But Ras got it too. One Sunday the preacher turned loose on the sins of the Casino [owned by Ras Wescott]. Now who is he talking about? I said.

In later years, I often stopped in to see Mama and Daddy after church and would tell them about hymns we sang. Daddy was always interested, and he tried to get Mama to go to church. But she only went a few times. She would say to Daddy, "Take care of your own soul, and I'll take care of mine."

FIGHT NIGHT

Daddy had one of the first radios—no one else in Manteo had one. "Ab" Wescott remembers how the men would come around to the house to hear fights on the radio every Friday night. You couldn't hear the radio too well, but people would look forward to "Fight Night" and would fill up our house.

Before the fights started, Daddy usually had music playing on the radio. One time they were playing the song, "Redwing," and when it was over, Mack Horney asked Daddy to play it again. Daddy told him that it wasn't possible to play it again—that you had to take what you get on the radio.

Ab heard Mack say that, and he says that he might have said it, too. No one but Daddy knew that the radio didn't work like a record player!

DADDY'S NEW STORE

The high tide came in lots of times and ruined the stock in Daddy's old waterfront store. Then the big fire in 1939 burned it down along with the other buildings on the waterfront.

So Daddy finally built a new store, and men from the store headquarters came to check on things and change the stock around every six months. For the first time in Daddy's store, there was a certain place for this or that.

My brother Moncie told Daddy that he would have to keep his desk straight and dress better. But Daddy wouldn't dress up for work. One time Moncie bought a new shirt for him from the Carson Davis Store, but Daddy refused to wear it as he said that it was too expensive. He took it to his store and sold it for less money than Moncie paid for it.

The men back then took grease from jars of "pom-pom" and rubbed so much on their hair that it would part in the back. Moncie put it on his hair and thought that Daddy should use it. But Daddy would have none of it. He said, "A louse will slip down the back of your head, and he'll break his neck sliding down the part!"

DADDY AND THE ABC

Women would beat up their men when they drank. When I was about 10 years old, Mama "cut a buck"—was so mad that she beat Daddy with a broom handle because he was drinking. I begged her to stop.

Another time Mama went to Daddy's store, grabbed everything off the shelves and let Daddy have it. He finally quit drinking because he said that he would not be able to get out of bed if he kept getting beatings.

Daddy was the first one to have the idea of ABC [state-controlled liquor stores] in Dare County, and he worked hard to get them here. Some folks were mad with him over it, but he thought that you couldn't stop people from drinking anyway, so the government might as well make some money out of it.

FIGHTING IN THE STREETS

There was one crew of men who would come along and start fights. That would clear the streets!

Daddy would run home and tell Mama to keep us children home when there was a fight brewing. Mama wasn't afraid—she would have liked to have gone and joined them.

Daddy said that there was a man who brought mail from Wanchese to Manteo in his two-seater surrey. The mail was in a little wooden box behind his seat. Sometimes he couldn't get out of town without a fight because some of the men would challenge him, and he would never run from a good fight.

On his way back to Wanchese, the mail-carrier often fell out in the marsh from his surrey because he had drunk too much firewater. His horse went on to Wanchese and delivered the mail right to the Post Office.

Drunks often went to sleep in the marsh. A snake never would bite them because they were pickled with all that alcohol!

SAVING DOLLARS

Daddy believed in saving dollars. He always said that he saved money every way that he could. Yellow was the cheapest paint so our house was painted that color every year.

My Model T was never sent to be repaired. Daddy would tell me to pump my brakes three times, and that would stop me. And it did for a long time.

But one day I was coming home from taking my brother Tommy for a ride in the Model T. When we were driving toward the garage, I pumped my brakes—but they gave way. The car broke down both doors and busted the back open. The garage wasn't ever repaired. It stayed that way for years.

In Ralph Swain's City Market one day, Daddy asked, "How much is this banana?" He saw some that were about rotten and was hoping that Ralph would give them to him. Ralph—who Daddy always said was a smart man—told him to help himself to the bananas.

While Daddy was interested in saving dollars, he was always known to be a most accommodating man and was especially good to the young crowd. He thought that they could do no wrong.

One time when "Ab" Wescott and John B. Etheridge were out in John's touring car, the brakes wouldn't take up, and they ran into Daddy's store. They went right over the curb and through a big glass window. Ab said that Daddy would never bill them or accept any money for damages.

THE BEACHCOMBER

Aunt Alwildy Culpepper, Daddy's half-sister, was the original beachcomber. Everybody called her that because she always combed the beach after storms and shipwrecks to see what she could find.

She couldn't wait to get to the beach after a storm. After she gathered up lumber there, her boys—Horatio, Hal and Sherman—would go to get it with a horse and cart.

Her house was built with lumber picked up off the beach. Aunt Alwildy lived at the foot of Jockey Ridge on the west side where she stayed until she got tired of sweeping sand out of her house. The sandhill began taking over the house so she had it moved over beside the ocean.

Aunt Alwildy also directed her boys to go into Nags Head Woods to gather mistletoe that she packed in barrels and sent to New

York. The people there sent the barrels right back filled with clothes in exchange for the mistletoe. Aunt Alwildy sold the clothes in her home—people came there to buy them. The clothes were lying on beds and chairs and all over the house. I remember a beautiful two-piece green dress that she gave me.

She also gathered berries, canned and preserved them, and sold those, too. There used to be lots of berries—locals picked them all the time during the season.

MANTEO COVERUP

In the 30's the town passed a rule that we had to be covered up if we walked downtown in a bathing suit. We had to have a coat on even though the bathing suits went down to our knees. However, the rule was never enforced with tourists and *Lost Colony* people as they brought in money.

Daddy and Mama were sitting on our porch one day when Mack Horney hopped off his porch across the street from them. He was wearing nothing but his swimming trunks and a straw hat. "Hi, Chief," he said to Daddy who used to be an engineer on the *Trenton*, the steamboat that brought passengers and merchandise into Manteo.

"Mack, where are you going with no clothes on? A cop will get you." Daddy said. And Mack replied with a lisp, "If the *Lost Colony* can do it, damned if Mack can't do it!"

One time Camille Brinkley, Hazel Willis, Iva Jennette and I took a skiff from Camille's shore and rowed out to the beacon that was off from the waterfront. We climbed on the beacon, jumped off and went swimming. While we were there, the weather changed suddenly. A storm came up and the waves turned over our skiff.

Preacher Hines was coming in from fishing so he picked us up and put us on the wharf. We hopped onto some gasoline barrels and were sitting there shivering, about to freeze to death in our wet bathing suits.

"Don't you dare get off those barrels," Cop Twiford came along and told us, "Or I'll arrest you!" Iva and Hazel waited for Iva's

Daddy to bring their coats, but Camille and I ran home bigtime—before the cop could catch us—because we didn't want to freeze.

SHOW BOAT

The Adams' came with the Show Boat in the early 30's. I never saw anything like it. It was something exciting!

Onstage they put on a live play with beautiful costumes and background. One of the plays was "Smilin' Through."

The Show Boat itself was just beautiful with red curtains and red cushioned seats. It was run by steam.

They came every summer to the Manteo waterfront for about four summers and stayed a week or two each time.

Adams' Show Boat was a place for dressing up, so everybody dressed up a lot when they went there. It was a bit of elegance that now is past.

BIG SHOWS

We put on shows that had a lot of music in them. They were held at the old schoolhouse where the bank parking lot is now.

My first husband Sheik [Alford] put on big shows that were put together well. In Elizabeth City, he played Rudolph Valentino and got the nickname Sheik.

I was in the Manteo shows before we were married. At 17, I was blacked up and wore pigtails—singing "Get out and under the moon!"

Rondal Lewark had a demijohn of white lightning and after getting into his jug, I danced as well as sang. I was feeling no pain!

Later—in the 40's—Dick Jordan put on blackface minstrel shows at the high school. He played the piano; Catherine Meekins and I sang and were all dressed up. I remember Jimmy Williams blacked up as an end man, cracking jokes and doing a lot of talking!

GRAVEYARD PRANK

Everyone knew how scared I was of messing around the dead. But one time Vernon Davis, Lessie Midgette and Camille Brinkley talked me into walking through the Manteo graveyard at night. I didn't want to be called "chicken" so I walked with them by all the stones though I was scared every step that I took.

I was holding on tight to my friends when all of a sudden Sheik, wearing a white sheet, rose up from behind Apollas Midgette's grave. His hands were in the air like someone coming up out of the ground. Sheik was a big man, too, like Paulas.

I was so shocked that I turned loose from holding my companions, and they ran away and left me. They had it all figured out just how to scare me!

VISITS TO THE DOCTOR

It was hard on the doctor in Manteo as he had all of the county to take care of when I was growing up. When people came to visit him, they had to come by boat and spend all day and the night somewhere, usually in homes of relatives.

It was often a combination visit—courthouse business as well as a visit to the doctor. The county seat was right here in Manteo. Court used to be held in the month of May.

All of my babies but one were born on the island, not in a hospital. Dr. Johnston, our doctor in Manteo, liked to deliver babies, and he delivered many of them. One time I needed him to deliver a baby, but he was at Hatteras Village [60 miles from Manteo] delivering twins. So a combination ambulance and hearse took me to Elizabeth City to the hospital. The road was a corduroy road with loose logs placed side by side across the marsh—it is no wonder that Della was born on the way!

I felt like I was on my last ride. If I had known that I was riding in a hearse, I *would* have died.

OLD TRANQUIL HOUSE

The old hotel was a pretty sight with big magnolia trees in the front yard and on each side, and with a big fig tree in back.

The Tranquil House was built by Mr. Chadwick from Elizabeth City. Mr. Gould—who came here with hunters from up north—bought the hotel in 1917. Earlier, he had built hunting clubs near Rodanthe and Bodie Island south of here.

Mr. Gould's wife Eliza ran the Tranquil House; he was not there much of the time as he was busy with the hunting clubs.

The Goulds had four daughters: Martha, Phoebe, Addie and Natalie. They all helped out in running the hotel. It was kept open year around.

Phoebe was 11 years old when they went to live there. She remembers a lot of hunters spending the night at the Tranquil House. Most of them came from up north. They started taking in drummers, too, at the hotel because there wasn't anywhere else to stay.

The old Tranquil House is gone now. It was torn down in the early 60's to make way for a new post office.

Phoebe married Dewey Hayman and went over to the beach at Nags Head where they ran the Arlington Hotel. She has been in the hospitality business all of her life!

HIGH TIDE

From boathouse to highway, there used to be only two houses on the side of the street where I live. When people began building houses around me, I told them to build up the land, but they didn't listen to me.

When we had a high tide one time, it was like a broom—it swept out everything. My neighbors down the street had to take every pot and pan they owned to throw water out of the windows of their house.

I told Miss Laura Hayman to move her car—that the tide was

coming in. But she just said, "Oh, Cora Mae," like I worried too much. The water went in her car windows so you know how high it got. She never drove that car again. It was ruined by the salt water and fell apart.

HARD TIMES

One of the worst times was after World War II. Things were so hard to get.

"Ab" Wescott, who was in the furniture business with his brothers, said that you couldn't get metal in any furniture right after the war. Also, if you wanted to build anything, you had to have a permit to get materials.

One time Ab promised a customer that he would get a metal bedstead for her. He always tried to accommodate his customers. A year later when he still didn't have the bedstead, he took down his wife Irlene's bed while she was gone and sold it to the customer.

Another time he took the regulator from the top of their gas tank and sold it. Irlene couldn't cook or have any hot water. She said that she was so mad that she didn't remember how mad!

LOST COLONY BEGINNINGS

When I was a little girl, Miss Mabel Evans started a show about the lost colonists at Ft. Raleigh. Miss Mabel had the time and know-how to take notice of our story. She put it all together, and someone from New York came to help put on the show for filming in a local movie. Natives and anybody else interested in the theater came to help—those who liked plays.

I have never forgotten the lullaby that we all sang in the play. We sang while we sat around a big iron pot and held imaginary babies in our arms. Miss Mabel told us to look out at the sound with the white caps coming in as we sang "Sweet and low, wind of the western sea, over the rolling waters go." So sweet.

The movie was shown at our local Pioneer Theater owned by the Creef Family. It is still shown there every year during special activities.

Later on, Paul Green came down with the idea of a play to be called *The Lost Colony*. He needed backing, so a group including Uncle Melvin, Martin Kellog and Bradford Fearing helped get it started. Uncle Melvin was so excited about the show going on.

Dottie and Sally and Sarah were the first of the family to go up there to be in the play. Dottie was an Indian squaw who carried a basket on her head and danced around the Indian king. Sally was an Indian dancer and Sarah was a milkmaid dancer.

They took along their little brother Marc, but he was only five years old, and it didn't work out for him to be up there. Later, another daughter, Della, was a principal character in the play. She was Dame Coleman for several years.

When Marc was seven years old, I took him along when there were tryouts for the play. In the courthouse, they had posted a list of those who were interested in trying out. Marc was not signed up as he said that he was still not interested in being in the play.

However, when he saw his friends going up on the stage, he went right on up there and was chosen. That made one mother mad as the devil—she was a firecracker! "You and your 'poly-tics'," she claimed.

Marc was good in the play. There was nothing shy about him. He spoke right up and had a nice voice.

PUTTING ON AIRS

During the time that Miss Mabel Evans was making a movie about the lost colonists, Mama was in it as a colonist lady. A reporter from a big city came by our house and asked Mama to take him to a rehearsal at Ft. Raleigh. Mama agreed to drive him although she had never taken the car out alone. Daddy had been trying to teach her to drive on Sundays.

Moncie and I hopped in the back seat of the touring car. The roads were crooked bridle-paths, and you had to ride on the side when cars were passing. Mama drove at a pretty big clip and we arrived safely at the fort entrance.

But as we turned into the fort, near the Virginia Dare Monument, Mama went down in a ditch that they had dug for Indians in one of the scenes. She grabbed the wheel and hollered, "Whoa, Whoa!"

That's what Mama got for putting on airs!

CLOWNING AROUND

At school is where I got started acting. I learned how to clown well to cover up the fact that I couldn't do 2 × 2.

I had a great phobia of figures and cut up all the time to hide it. Even the teachers didn't know about it. When we had a beauty contest at school, I won because they all liked me, not because I was pretty!

At Daddy's store I never wanted to mess with the cash register or have anything to do with figures. One day my schoolteacher Miss Essie Wescott saw me at the store and wanted me to measure three yards of material for her. I had to tell her that I couldn't do it. She was surprised and didn't understand.

After I was married, I bought a book on doing figures, but it made me nervous, and I shut up the book. Not being able to do 2 × 2 has made me feel insecure in life, but when I joined *The Lost Colony*, I fit right in—"Cora Mae the Clown". No one there would have ever believed that I had an insecure feeling.

UNCLE MELVIN DANIELS

My Uncle Melvin was an unusual person. He always said, "Go to bed with a clear conscience and live by the golden rule."

During the 52 years that he was Register of Deeds, he always helped the old people. He took plenty of time in helping them find their land recorded in the county books and would only charge them a dollar. "The good Lord meant for you to help the widows," he said.

One time two new lawyers right from college came in the courthouse and jumped on him and said that he would have to start charging people more. But Uncle Melvin didn't pay any attention to the lawyers.

In the early years of *The Lost Colony*, Uncle Melvin always was the guest speaker on the 18th of August, Virginia Dare's birthday. Dare County night—when the locals got in free—used to be on August 18th.

One night Uncle Melvin was speaking there at *The Lost Colony*. A young man named Bobby, who was studying to be a preacher, was so impressed with the speech that Uncle Melvin was giving. Bobby went backstage and told all the young people, "Listen to this old man talk; he murders the English language to death, but it's beautiful the history he can tell."

They all went and listened to him and were so calm and quiet. Uncle Melvin could charm a snake!

THE LOST COLONY—RAIN OR SHINE

I enjoyed every moment—backstage as well as onstage—when I was in *The Lost Colony* cast. Those were the happiest days of my life.

I even enjoyed playing in a storm. It was in our contracts that we would act in rain or shine. If it was raining, we kept playing as long as the audience stayed in their seats. Then the houselights were turned up when it was time for us to stop.

One night Old Tom and I made three entrances to the parapet, trying to finish a scene. Tommy Hull was acting the part of Old Tom. Every time that he started saying the same speech, the houselights would go up as it was raining again and blowing a storm. The guests began laughing, and it was so funny that Tommy began singing a rain song, adding to the merriment.

Rennie [Irene Rains], the costumer, would sit through storms at her sewing machine with rain coming in through a door backstage. But it didn't bother her—she is a down-homer like the rest of us on Roanoke Island.

I would go and sit on a bench behind the theater and watch the sound during storms. Two of the locals who played colonist roles, Cora Twiford and Maxine Peele, would tell me to come inside—that I would get soaking wet and be struck by lightning!

Sometimes new cast members became upset and nervous when the rain was beating against us, and the wind was blowing hard. One young man came around with a petition saying that we would not act in bad weather. I said to him, "I love a storm—I am as old as your grandmother, and I can do it." That fellow didn't get many signatures for his petition and was blackballed the next year.

ANDY—A GOOD DADDY

Andy Griffith's children Dixie and Sammy were both in *The Lost Colony* for several years. That's how we got to see Andy so much. He would come backstage to visit with us and to check on his children.

One time I watched Hunt—Marjalene Thomas' son—and Andy's little boy Sammy playing a trick on another boy. They exchanged his prop for somebody else's in the play. He ran in the dark and grabbed the wrong prop and got into trouble when the director saw him.

Andy saw me getting after Sammy and Hunt and said to me, "I know my boy's done something wrong—what is it?" But I said, "If the boys don't straighten up, I'll come tell you. If they apologize, you won't hear about it." And Andy never did.

FALSE TEETH CAPER

The children in *The Lost Colony* really could not be blamed for playing tricks on one another because they saw us grownups doing it.

Tommy Hull who played Old Tom loved to play tricks the same as I. During the Virginia Dare christening scene, he would run down the ramp by me and would get close to my ear and squall "Hear ye, hear ye!" It made bells in my ear.

I couldn't get him to stop, so I decided to get even by putting false teeth in a mug used in a scene with Old Tom. Everything was planned out with the help of another actor who played John Borden.

Two mugs were used in the scene. Onstage John Borden passed them to me, and I was supposed to pass them to Old Tom. I handed one to him, and he drank from it. Then I passed him the one with the teeth in it and grinned to show that my upper plate was missing!

Old Tom couldn't drink from that mug when he saw those teeth and was so excited that he flipped it in the air. It hit Fernando the Spaniard who couldn't keep from laughing though he was supposed to have a stern look.

My own upper plate was safely tucked in my bosom. I never play games with *my* teeth!

LADY BIRD'S VISIT

During intermission, Lady Bird Johnson came backstage at *The Lost Colony* to meet us. I told her, "I have Texas dirt on my face right now!" We actually did have Texas soil in our makeup.

I also told her that I was proud of her beautification projects. Not long before, I had read about how she was helping to save the redwood forest in California. "Nicest compliment I've had here," she said. She was ready to talk more, but she had to go get her seat as the play was about to start again.

RESCUING THE LOST COLONY

In 1964 *The Lost Colony* was in the red. Dr. Fred and Mrs.

Morrison stepped in to help us by going to New York to get Joe Layton for our director.

Joe came in, cut a few lines and scenes, and changed to night rehearsals. I liked the change because there was a nice cool breeze at night, and the moonlight was pretty on the water. Sometimes in the daytime rehearsals, it was so hot that I thought I was going to pass out.

We rehearsed for two weeks before the show started. Joe worked everyone to death till they got it right—he was real good.

I enjoyed watching Joe direct the dancers who had such perfect rhythm. When he directed the prologue where the group comes in and sings at the beginning of the play, the members looked like they were coming up out of the earth. It was a world of fantasy appearing as though the sky was turning dark and clouds rolling in.

Joe also brought in the best lights we could get; Nan Porcher could turn them into beautiful shades.

Bob Knowles, the hardest worker I ever saw there, was trained by Joe Layton. Bob knew how to keep the show going after Joe left town and went back to New York each year after rehearsals. No one could ever beat Bob Knowles—he never ran out of energy.

AN ARCHITECT'S DREAM

Manteo was going dead when Mayor John Wilson came in and envisioned a cultural center downtown. I saw the biggest improvement in no time—you couldn't recognize the place!

John had in his mind the idea of what he wanted for the town. First, he fixed up an old building into a pretty tudor style—that didn't cost the town a cent. Then he worked on his grandfather's house, the old Jones' place. It is beautiful the way he remodeled it.

The new Tranquil House on the waterfront was designed by John. It's beautiful, too, and an asset to the town.

John also had the idea to have low-income housing [Scarborough Town]. He was all for it, but he didn't want the houses just slapped up side by side. Wherever John goes, beauty goes.

I like an old Chinese proverb that I read years ago: if you have two coins, spend one for a loaf of bread and one for a flower bulb. You need to have beauty in life.

THE NEW WATERFRONT

There is a pretty view now where there once was a rundown waterfront. And you can sit on benches or visit nice shops.

The park beside the waterfront condos is pretty, too, that Jule Burrus got going. I have enjoyed helping him weed flowers there. Land for the park was given by the Creef family.

Moored at Ice Plant Island, the Elizabeth II is a wonderful ship, teaching us our heritage and tying in with the *Lost Colony*.

Old Sir Walter Raleigh—the wooden statue—is a popular landmark downtown, but the woodpeckers have about got him!

MOUNTAIN HILL

We used to have Easter egg hunts on a big sandhill called Mountain Hill on the north end of Roanoke Island. Every Easter Monday, we cooked up great bunches of eggs and met other families there. It was a playground for all.

Andy Griffith owns the property now where Mountain Hill stood, but it is mostly wooded now.

A lot of the big sandhills on Roanoke Island have been bulldozed down. I wonder why people take down trees and hills. It seems like everything has been bulldozed down.

LOVE OF OUTDOORS

Our skies used to be covered with ducks and geese. I have always loved to listen to geese honking when they were coming down from the north.

I remember big flocks flying overhead while I was hanging out clothes. There were geese not twenty feet over my head—headed to the Brinkley Marsh.

We have lost a lot of beauty here. I think that pesticides have killed off much of our wildlife. DDT was one of the worst things to hit the Outer Banks.

The good Lord gave us this world! Every night I say a prayer for the Park Service. If they hadn't come along, we would have little left of nature's beauty.

I love the outdoors and often think of a favorite poem learned long ago......*The Sandpiper* by Celia Thaxter.

> Across the narrow beach we flit,
>   One little sandpiper and I
> And fast I gather, bit by bit,
>   The scattered driftwood bleached and dry.
> The wild waves reach their hands for it,
>   The wild wind raves, the tide runs high,
> As up and down the beach we flit,—
>   One little sandpiper and I.

MANTEO MEMORIES
[photos from family and friends]

THEODORE MEEKINS—1914
with Jerry—the shipwrecked dog
[photo courtesy of Goldie Meekins]

CAPT. THOMAS & SARAH MIDGETTE
Mama's parents

BENJAMIN & SARAH DANIELS
Daddy's parents

MAMA IN HER BATHING SUIT – 20's
a funny-looking sight

MARJORIE BAUM — 20's
on father's oil truck

DADDY'S TUG & OIL TANKS-20's
downtown Manteo

CORA MAE & FRIENDS—20's
having fun

POP AND HIS TOURING CAR—20's
on *Sunday afternoon outing*

EASTER EGG HUNT—early 30's
on *Mountain Hill*

LESSIE—20's
out for a good time

CORA MAE WITH BROTHER TOMMY
ready to ride my pony

SHOW BOAT—1930
a bit of elegance

DOWNTOWN MANTEO—20's
heading for Daddy's store

[photos courtesy of Irlene Wescott]

BESSIE LANE, MARJORIE & BALFOUR - 1918
Wash Baum's children
[photo courtesy of Marjorie Baum Wescott]

FIRST BRIDGE TO NAGS HEAD - 1927
where we beat the toll
[photo courtesy of Chief Hatton Midgett]

OLD TRANQUIL HOUSE-1920
a pretty sight
[photo courtesy of Doris Bonner]

BOATHOUSE ON DOUGH'S CREEK
much photographed view in Manteo
[photo courtesy of Ab Wescott]

MAMA & FRIENDS—1951
a good fishing day

MAMA & ROCKFISH—1951
happy when fishing

DADDY—MONCIE L. DANIELS, SR.
loved by all

MABEL EVANS—1921
in old movie about colonists

AGONA & OLD TOM—1959
my first Old Tom [Ray Smith]

CORA MAE & ELOISE McCAIN—1983
with my best understudy

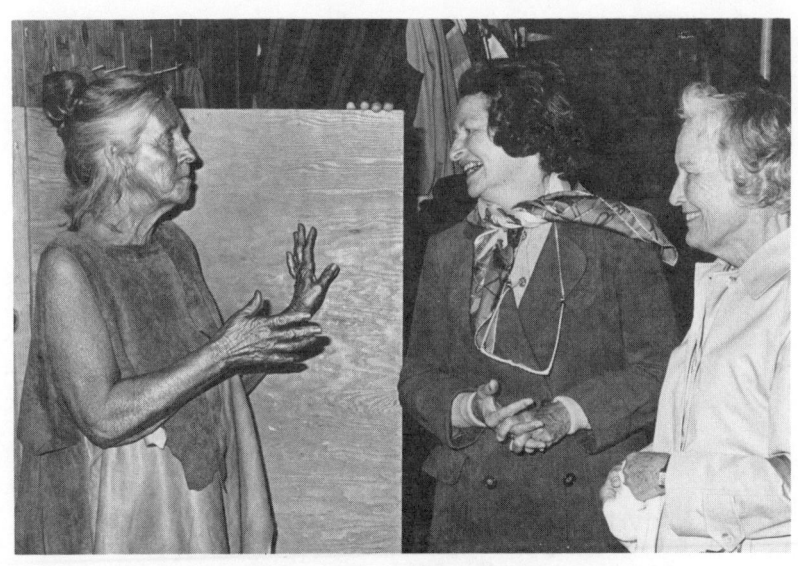

LADY BIRD & MRS. FRED MORRISON
visiting with Agona backstage
[photo by Foster Scott]

PAUL GREEN & AGONA
with author of THE LOST COLONY
[photo by Foster Scott]

June 28/

Dear Cora Mae --

Now that you are reaching almost a quarter of a century in the part of "Agona," as author of "The Lost Colony," I want to thank you a thousand times for your long and joyful service.

Affectionately,
Paul Green.

MODERN MANTEO

CORA MAE'S BRIDGE
leading to Ice Plant Island

ELIZABETH II
docked at Ice Plant Island

SIR WALTER RALEIGH
surveying many changes